Group Benefits Exposed

How to Save Money, Reduce Taxes, and Increase Employee Productivity

Douglas G.R. Pinnell

Group Benefits Exposed

Published by:
90-Minute Books
302 Martinique Drive
Winter Haven, FL 33884
www.90minutebooks.com

Copyright © 2015, Douglas G.R. Pinnell

Published in the United States of America

ISBN-13: 978-0692561850
ISBN-10: 0692561854

For more information on 90-Minute Books including finding out how you can
publish your own lead generating book, visit www.90minutebooks.com or call
(863) 318-0464

Here's What's Inside

Introduction

In over 15 years of working with business owners, I've noticed that many aren't getting the maximum value from their group benefits plans. In many cases, benefits plan costs increase year after year, payroll costs continue to grow, and tax strategies are not maximized.

When Firm Principals, HR staff, and other Key Decision-Makers understand how a good benefits program can improve their bottom line, the monies spent on group benefits packages become an investment rather than an expense.

My goal in writing this book is to expose some of the myths about group benefits plans. In my experience, it's an unfortunate reality that some insurance advisors keep consumers in the dark about how benefits plans work. This often leads to higher costs, a low return on employee payroll costs, and distrust between the advisor and the business owner. When all the parties truly understand their plan, they can start working as a team to everyone's greatest benefit.

I hope this book educates you on the true value your benefits program adds to your company's bottom line.

Here's to Your Continued Success!

Douglas G.R. Pinnell

PART ONE – How to Get More from Your Group Benefits Investment

Group Benefits 101

In this chapter we will talk about the basics of group benefits plans.

While Canadians have an amazing health care program that lets us see a doctor or go to the hospital anytime, anywhere, once we are outside the doctor's office or the hospital, we are on our own.

For example, we have to pay for the medicines the doctor prescribes*, we pay for follow up and "non-medical" treatments like physiotherapy and other costs.

To help balance budgets Provincial governments have also delisted many services over the years, pushing costs back to us. For example, we now have to pay for ambulance rides, eye checkups, etc. Of course, dental services have always been pay as you go.

A sudden medical or dental problem could cost thousands of dollars that most people are not prepared to handle.

Having a health and dental plan is one way to protect you from these sudden and expensive situations.

There are two basic categories of these: "Individual" and "Group" plans.

As the name suggests, individual plans are intended for individuals to buy for themselves and their families. These plans are discretionary i.e. you choose to buy or not. The majority of programs are "medically underwritten." This means you have to provide health information to qualify for coverage.

Accordingly, if you or someone in your family already has a health issue (high blood pressure, a child with asthma, etc.,) the insurer will likely apply exclusions or limitations related to the pre-existing condition. They may even decline to offer coverage if the condition is severe enough.

This is somewhat analogous to car insurance. You wouldn't expect to get coverage for damage already on a car, nor would you expect to be able to buy Insurance when you are already in the ditch after an accident.

While guaranteed issue plans are available, they are generally very limited.

One exception is some companies offer plans to people who have just lost coverage through an employer group plan. Generally these must be purchased within 30 to 60 days of the employee losing their benefits. These commonly still have some limits, in particular related to drug coverage.

I sometimes hear complaints regarding premium costs compared to the expenses paid. Folks will say "I only spend about $X why would I pay $Y for an insurance program?" In my experience, health and dental programs are the only insurance where people not only want to claim but think they should take more out than goes in.

This thought process ignores the insurance aspect of these plans. Once insured, if something happens in the future, the plan could pay 2, 3, or more times what was paid in, while the affected person still only pays the regular premium amount. There are also potential tax advantages over paying "out of pocket."

Employer based group plans generally do not ask health questions. This is because all employees are enrolled so the "risk" is shared across the whole company.

Employers are able to work with their insurance broker to structure the plan effectively, determining what is covered and the service limits. For example, what percentage of drug claims, annual maximums for eyeglasses, paramedical services like physiotherapy and massage and of course the type and amount of dental services. Once established the insurer agrees to pay up to these limits and publishes a booklet stipulating this. If you calculated the amount people could potentially claim, it would add up to hundreds if not thousands of dollars more than even the most expensive plan.

Additional coverages like Disability and Critical Illness can also be included on the plan. Again, medical evidence may not be required. The size of the group creates limits on these guarantees called non-evidence maximums (NEM) more on that topic to follow!

In a nutshell, employers have to find a balance between what is covered and the cost of the plan. Plan costs are reviewed annually.

The "everyone into the pool" nature of group plans provides a level of rate stability as not everyone makes big claims every year; the larger the group the greater the stability. High usage does drive up the rate paid. Rate increases are not to make up for the past but to help the insurer protect against losses going forward.

Two other primary advantages of employer based plans are the fact that employers pay some if not all of the premiums for their employees, which is a benefit to the employee over having to pay everything for themselves. Even better, the amount the employer pays is a non-taxable benefit to the employee. And of course claims are always non-taxable. This is one of those rare "everyone wins" situations.

To summarize:

1) The employer pays and writes off the full premium as a business expense.

2) Employees do not pay any tax on the premium employers pay for them. A raise or reimbursement by an employer, however, would be fully taxable.

3) Claims, employees make, are just paid (reimbursed) by the plan. One could claim thousands of dollars and would still not pay any taxes on the amount claimed.

Note: Tax laws change and vary by region so make sure you speak to your accountant regarding any tax related issues.

How to Avoid Being Taken Advantage Of

Business owners believe that they're being taken advantage of by everyone involved in insurance. In their defense, in some cases they are. They may believe their employees are taking advantage of them because "they're the ones who make all those claims which push their cost up every year!" They may think the insurers are taking advantage of them by the fact that they always seem to be increasing the prices. In my experience, I find it's not uncommon that the clients themselves don't understand Benefits 101—the basic model of "money in, money out." The more that goes out, the more that needs to go in!

The adversarial mindset is often due to how advisors present the benefits package to the business owner. Often they simply tell them, "Here's your coverage, here's your renewal this year. See you later." They don't break down the numbers with them. They don't justify the existence of the plan so the business owners understand what they are paying for and the direct effect it has on employee morale and productivity. The employers only see all the claims and the fees. If they see the claims are way up, they think the staff is abusing the plan. Note: Sometimes they are.

Think about car insurance as an example, something that everybody knows about and everybody hears stories about. How frequently do you hear about someone who has an accident and then their rates increase? They'll say, "I've driven for twenty years and never had a problem. Why does one accident overrule that?"

That's all they see. It's in your coffee break conversations. Claims go up, rates go up. When someone takes the time to sit down and explain how the claims are going up and you understand what the employees are using it for, you don't have the same frustration with yearly increases.

When I meet with businesses about the renewal of their group benefits plan and I tell them their rates are going up, they're never happy about it; don't get me wrong. But when they understand where the numbers are coming from they understand that I've worked hard with them, and with the insurers, over the years to make sure that they're not paying excessively. People with other advisors may think: I pay, I pay, I pay. I don't use, I don't use, I don't use. Then, all of a sudden, I do use my policy and they make me pay more. If they know as they're going along that they're paying a reasonable amount based on what's coming back out, they understand the numbers. Then, when there is an increase, there's a causative link between those two items. It's not just take, take, take on the part of the carriers.

Part of the problem that people don't understand about Canadian insurance is that when someone has an accident, they're more likely to have another. This doesn't hold for everyone, but it's not uncommon. You may have heard about or known someone who had an accident. They rear-ended somebody or were rear-ended by someone else and then you're talking to them six months or a year later and it happened again.

It's more common than you think. Many people drive differently for a while. They're now nervous. They're not trying to be dangerous but maybe they are over-cautious and do something out of the ordinary. Most advisors won't explain that to the client either. The client says, "Well, yeah, but I drove safely for twenty years. I should be good for another twenty." Maybe YOU will, but a statistically significant amount won't.

Why Education Is the Key to Saving Money

A number of years ago, I was brought in to help a company who was unhappy about their rates. Their paramedical claims (chiropractic, massage therapy, etc.) had doubled for three years running. They went from twelve thousand dollars' worth of claims to twenty-four thousand dollars' worth of claims to forty-eight thousand dollars' worth of claims within the same firm. As a result, their rates also doubled each time. That's when they called me: when they were about to double for the third time. I went in and took a look at what was going on and I talked to them. By digging into it and understanding how their rates worked, I was actually able to get the insurer to agree that the claims could not double again. They had maxed out!

There are limits on how much people can claim for these services. In this case once I did the math, and considered the number of people involved, it was clear that they couldn't claim much more. In other words, their claims for paramedical were as high as they could possibly go. They didn't have to double the rates again as a result. That was the first piece I was able to get them to sit up and notice. Next, we put in a bit of direct cost sharing with the employees, so when the employees were using this service, they understood that there was an impact. When people think lunch is free, they'll eat everything

When the benefits are free, sometimes people think that they should try to get as much as they possibly can out of it. They want to use it to the absolute maximum that's available rather than what is needed.

The third thing that I was able to do, for this client, was educating the staff. I had the owner give me a couple of hours to speak directly with the staff. I went through the plan itself to show them what was covered, but I also explained the concept of money in and money out. Up until then, they had thought they were sticking it to the insurance company by taking all these "free" services. They liked that idea and thought the group benefits services were free, and people like free stuff.

The next year, after explaining that these services were not in fact, "free", their claims dropped dramatically. Accordingly, I was able to bring the rates down the subsequent year. The first year I significantly reduced the costs from the rate at which they were initially going to renew with the other broker by recognizing they had maxed out the rates at the previous year's level. The subsequent year, I brought them down again because people started appreciating what they had rather than abusing it.

A key part of our business model is a requirement that whenever I set up a group I must be allowed to make a presentation to the staff. When the employees are educated about what a benefits plan really is, the abuse stops and people have a new-found respect for the value that the company is providing to them.

Sure, some employees don't want to be told the truth. I have had people in the room say, "Well, the booklet says I can spend five hundred dollars on massages and five hundred dollars on chiropractic and five hundred dollars on physiotherapy and five hundred dollars on acupuncture. So I'm going to!"

We call these people the abusers. If that's the employee's attitude, odds are that employer has more issues with them than just the group benefits.

The purpose of a benefits plan is for people to use it to look after themselves so that little problems don't become big problems. It also ensures that when there is a big problem, there's a safety net. It is not intended to be used to the maximums that are available, just because they can be.

Why Group Benefits Are an Investment Direct to Your Bottom Line

When you understand that reducing turnover and increasing productivity leads to a better bottom line, you understand that it is more important to have the right plan than just to have the lowest price. When you understand how rates are determined, you are more inclined to work with the advisor and insurer for solutions. You also see the insurer's efforts to ensure that claims are legitimate as a way to help control costs rather than trying not to pay. (In fact, the more they pay, the more they can charge; which is in the insurers favour.)

When staff members are educated about how things work they have an increased appreciation for the plan and the employer that provides it to them. In my experience, they become more of a partner. This leads to a less self-centred attitude, which is good for the employer and its bottom line.

My passion is to help business owners sleep at night knowing they are getting the best value for their money and that their priorities are looked after without the added stress of unnecessary conflicts.

Why Group Benefits Are the Only Kind of Insurance People Want to Use

If you own a car, you have and pay for car insurance. We pay our car insurance knowing that it's there if we need to use it, but we hope to heck it's never necessary. It's the same thing with life insurance. We buy it but we pray we will never need it.

Health benefits plans are the only insurance product where people want to claim on it and want to claim more than they paid for it.

Health insurance is seen from a different paradigm. With life insurance, car insurance, etc., you don't want to ever have to file a claim. You don't want to ever have to have your house rebuilt after it burned down, but you have the insurance there and you just pay the money. You know it's there. With health benefits, some people think, "I paid for it, it says it will cover all this, therefore I must use these services." You never say to yourself, "I have car insurance, so I should go out and smash my car up so I can get a new one."

That's the way a lot of people treat their health benefits—until they are educated and understand how it all works. As I always say in my presentations, "The insurance is there. If you need it, use it. If you slip and fall and you hurt yourself and you need physiotherapy, or you need to go to a chiropractor, I don't think anyone in this room would begrudge your making claims on that even if it increased the rates." It's pretty hard for people to sit in a room and say, "Yeah, if you're hurt I would want you to not use this."

When you explain it to them that way, they get it. But if people found out that you were using it just because it's there (and as a result their price went up), then they would be upset. Group benefits are there for when you need them but they are not intended to be abused.

How to Increase Employee Productivity

In my company, we are always looking for superstars to join our team. These individuals are aligned with our core values so we know we can count on them to provide quality customer service, work hard to keep our clients, and be constantly on the lookout for new ways to help us operate more profitably. On more than one occasion we have been in a competitive situation when hiring staff; having a competitive group benefits plan has helped us bring some talented people onboard.

In any size of business, employee turnover has a significant cost. It's often a hidden cost which can quickly add up. For example, when someone leaves, you have to run ads to hire a replacement. You may also have to pay a head hunter, and fees etc. You have to spend <u>your time</u> interviewing (which means you aren't being paid for what you are best at doing!), and of course training is a huge time investment, not to mention documenting all of your core business practices.

As a result, the average cost to replace someone is in the several-thousand-dollar range. If the employee left to work for a firm with group benefits, you may find yourself thinking that the cost of your own group plan is not that expensive. If you took the turnover costs and allocated them toward the group plan, you might find that you are actually ahead of the game.

The Trends That Directly Affect Your Group Benefits Costs

One of the big trends that are affecting benefits plans is that people are living longer. There are new medications and new treatments coming out all the time. If you turn the clock back a hundred years or so, the biggest causes of death were: bad water, food and the flu. We don't die of those things anymore. You eat some bad shrimp at a restaurant, you go home and you're sick for a couple of days. Nowadays, we have heart-related issues from all the stresses we are exposed to, such as the chemicals in our foods, which lead to cancers. The focus of expenditures has changed dramatically.

As the baby boomer generation gets older, we are placing immense amounts of pressure on the system. The reality is the average life expectancy used to be, depending on how far you turn the clock back, forty to fifty years. Now, people are expecting to live into their mid-eighties and beyond. No one used to plan to live to ninety-five. There were some people that made it, but no one planned for that. Now many people live that long or longer.

Because we are living longer, our bodies have a greater chance of breaking down. Earlier, I mentioned those old cars. They break down. They've been around a long time. The machine just wears out a little bit as time progresses. There are things you can do to help minimize that wearing out. That's where a lot of the group plans come in because they have some maintenance options in place. Benefits plans allow access to chiropractic and massage treatment and getting your dental work done on a regular basis so you don't end up needing a root canal. Your teeth don't rot out of your mouth because you're getting them looked after on a regular basis. These are things that people didn't need in the past because they didn't live as long.

In a perfect world, no one gets sick and everyone has perfect teeth. Then there's the real world. In the real world, people do get sick. People do want to look after themselves, and people do have issues with their teeth. Money is spent on that. One way or another, before you get any money to spend on those services, you're giving a piece of it to somebody. For example, you go to the dentist and you need a root canal and they want a thousand dollars. If you have to pay for it yourself, you have to come up with that money. You have to go to work and earn fifteen hundred to two thousand dollars in order to have a thousand dollars in the bank, after taxes, to give to the dentist.

The other option is some form of service provider doing it for you. You're giving them a piece of that five hundred to a thousand dollars instead of the tax man. You're still going to pay for those services. The question is, "Which is the more effective, more efficient, way of paying for those services?" I submit that a group program which collects the money that employees and employers are spending anyway is better than giving it all to the government. There are also tax mechanisms, but they don't have any sort of safety net. That's the other problem with a pay as you go model. When you get sick, you have to pay. If you get really sick, you have to pay a lot.

Having some sort of true insurance model in place where maybe you pay a portion of it, but then if something goes really wrong, there's something there to cover it. There's the fully insured model where, just like with your car insurance, most years you're going to pay more money in than you take out. Sometimes you put *significantly* more money in than you take out. That's where that animosity thing comes in again. "Wait a minute. I gave you a thousand dollars and we only spent three hundred dollars. You took seven hundred bucks." No one ever remembers the year where they paid a thousand dollars and spent three.

The idea is that very rarely would you only pay a thousand and claim three. If it's being managed properly, you're going to pay a thousand dollars and you're going to claim eight hundred dollars. Expecting that, obviously, you have to pay something to somebody. That's going to continue. Those times when you claimed three thousand, several other people paid two hundred dollars, to cover your overuses that year. That's how all insurance works. Everyone pays a little so that there are dollars available for those that need a lot.

The key to proper management at the broker's level, or the insurer's level, is good education on the employee's level so they're not abusing it in any way. If someone gets cancer, the costs are the costs. Generally speaking, as I said earlier, no one is going to begrudge the fact that you spent a ton of money on medication to help you fight your battle with cancer. People will be unhappy if they find out that the reason their rates went up is the fact that you really like massages and go for them just because they're covered.

If the numbers have been managed properly all along, then when there's a bad year, you're bound to take an increase. If it's done right and if the broker is on your side, then we mitigate what that increase is going to be. No one took the full brunt of the preceding year in the way that employee would have if there was no safety net in place. Our healthcare program in Canada is very good for the "get sick, go to the hospital", portion of it. Anybody can go to any hospital anywhere in the country anytime. They get hurt or they get sick, it gets looked after. All the medications while they're in the hospital are looked after. All the nurses and doctors coming to see them are covered.

As soon as they walk out of the building, they're on their own tab. When a patient walks out of the building with a prescription for heart medications after having just had bypass surgery or a stroke, they buy that medication out of their own pocket one way or another for as long as necessary. The group programs are a way to take that cost again and scatter it across the three people, the thirty people, the three hundred people, in the company instead of just the patient's pocket.

That's the basics of insurance, period. Everybody puts in a dollar so that, when someone needs to, they can reach in with both hands and take out money by the fistful.

Covering the Essentials Cost Effectively

All group programs have at least a nominal life insurance benefit. Employers decide the value of that insurance. If any employee does pass away, there's money available to their family. A lot of group plans have disability insurance. Disability insurance is what I call a paycheque replacer. If someone can't work due to injury or illness, the insurance company steps in and replaces the paycheque for as long as that person is unable to work.

Health and dental insurance is included in most benefits packages. Dental is straightforward. You can get check-ups and cleanings so your teeth are maintained. If something goes wrong, no matter how well you maintain them, and you end up needing a root canal, it'll pay for a root canal. You can add on coverage for more sophisticated costs such as crowns, bridges, dentures, orthodontics, or cosmetic treatments as well. They do add to the cost on the program.

On the health insurance side, there's coverage available for everything from drugs to an upgraded hospital room. You're covered here in Canada if you go to the hospital, but ward rooms can have four to eight people in them. You can pay a couple hundred dollars a day extra to be upgraded to a semi-private or a private room. Group benefits plans frequently will cover the cost of that upgraded room.

"Paramedical services" i.e. chiropractic, massage therapy, physiotherapy are services that can help someone if they slip and fall and they torque their knee, or hurt their back. With this added coverage, you can get treatment related to getting back on your feet.

Massage therapy is part of a lot of plans. If you get massage therapy just because you like it, that's not the best reason for doing so. If the reason you're getting massages is the fact that while sitting at a computer for hours on end you end up with a tense neck and tension headaches, it is a soft cost. Without massage, you might have more sick days. You might get up and leave your desk more often. You might be sitting there holding your head with tension headaches, hurting your neck, which is not productive.

In my experience, paying for that person to have a massage, even if it pushes your rates up for everybody, is a worthwhile investment. Putting in that money actually gets you more productivity. It provides a greater amount of money than the cost of the benefits plan itself. If you're paying someone $100 a day but they're only working at eighty percent efficiency, you're actually costing yourself $20 a day (approximately $5,000 per year!). Compare that to the cost of your benefits plan and you will likely find the investment in benefits is worthwhile.

If you can have the employee work, at a hundred percent, by spending that twenty dollars on proactive treatments, you might actually get a hundred and twenty dollars' worth of value from them or more. Often, you normally wouldn't pay them a hundred dollars a day to only generate a hundred dollars of value. They're generating ten times or more of the value for the money you're paying them for the time they're putting in. It's very worthwhile from that perspective because they actually make a difference in how you function. Those employees will reward you with higher productivity and fewer sick days.

From an employer's perspective—going back to the life insurance and the disability insurance and even the health insurance, the drug coverage that I referred to as well—it kind of correlates to the car insurance example where people say, "Well, I had no problems for years and then something happened." Perhaps you have an employee who works for you for a number of years and who then gets sick or hurt. Obviously, an employer cannot afford to pay an employee who isn't showing up to work. That's a given and a pretty straightforward one. It would be unfortunate to have an employee who worked for a number of years who got sick or hurt and couldn't work, and you didn't have disability insurance in place. Everybody feels sorry for the employee, but at some level or other it's not uncommon that other employees think that you should be doing something for that individual. They hear the story, through the grapevine, about how he's struggling. The family is in trouble because they can't afford to pay their mortgage. It's a not uncommon thought that the employer should be doing something about that. People may dismiss the thought afterwards. "What could they do?" But it's still there. Someone gets sick and needs medications. The employee comes back to work and he's talking about his heart condition. Now he's on three hundred dollars' a month of medication.

It's not reasonable to think the employer should suddenly give that person thirty-six hundred dollars a year more than anybody else either. People don't look at it that way. The group plan with the disability insurance, as an example, provides a way for the employer to give the employee a paycheque when they're not coming to work. It's just not <u>their</u> cheque.

It's a way that they can make sure that person is getting the needed medications while they're fighting cancer or dealing with their heart condition and so on. Everybody on the team is sharing that cost one way or another through a group plan which is not the case when it's a pay as you go, every man for himself situation.

To Reduce Your Taxes

With or without a Group Plan there are a couple of solutions you may be able to use to enhance the program or at least save some tax money on services you already have.

1) A Health Spending Account (HSA) can be added to a traditional plan or even set up on a standalone basis. These "Health Chequing Accounts" as I like to explain them are NOT an Insurance solution. They can be a great tax-mechanism. Simply explained, much like your personal or business chequing account you deposit

money into it and when there is money there, you can "write cheques" against it.

With a HSA you decide on an annual and/or monthly contribution amount for yourself as the owner and/or for your staff. If you need dental services, a prescription filled, new glasses, etc. you pay for the required service then submit for a "reimbursement" cheque from the HSA. When added to a plan the annual contribution amount increases the employers cost but can give added flexibility to employees as it can cover things the plan does not or supplement what it does.

These can be set up on a "stand alone' basis creating a way for a business owner to effectively convert personal health expenses to a business expense. Since Business tax rates are generally lower than personal this can translate to a significant savings; especially on larger items e.g. orthodontics for yourself or your children, care for a disabled child or other close family member, etc.

Again, this is not insurance so if something catastrophic happens there is no risk sharing so you "only" get the tax savings. Note: a few Insurers offer Catastrophic Medical Expense insurance that could be added to an HSA. This is sometimes called "Stop Loss" protection, as it stops you having to pay (losing more money) above a pre-set level. You are still on your own for the first few thousand dollars but if you got Cancer, etc. this could be the difference between having care and going broke! Of course there is a cost to put this insurance in place that has to be considered.

2) "Cost Plus" is a feature available on Traditional Benefits plans. Similar to a HSA,

it is not insurance and its value is in the tax savings. Whereas a HSA requires some sort of set annual or monthly contribution, Cost Plus claims are more "pay as you go." The braces mentioned earlier could be claimed when they happen vs. being "planned for" as you would do with a HSA.

The Tax Man (Person) has rules related to how these are to be used so you have to be careful not to run afoul of him/her!

NOTE: Again, there is no free lunch. Both have admin fees but they are usually much lower than your income tax rate making these worth consideration.

Avoiding Costly Mistakes

I had a client who, when they first approached me, had a group benefits program that was not set up properly. One of the owners in this particular case was very sick. It turns out that because the plan wasn't properly structured, he didn't have the life insurance he was supposed to have and he didn't have the amount of disability insurance he was supposed to have. In fact, when I first stepped in, the insurer felt he had neither of those.

I was able to make some changes to the contract to which the insurer agreed, although they didn't have to. This was because I had experience and a good relationship with the company. They could have refused under the rules of the contract as they existed at the time of the illness. He should have had several thousand dollars a month of disability insurance, and he should have had a couple hundred thousand dollars of life insurance. In the end, he ended up only getting a couple thousand dollars a month in disability and about fifty thousand or so on the life insurance side—all because it hadn't been set up properly.

The core issue here is that my client hadn't had his plan properly designed. Because the firm had a complex business structure, the group benefits plan needed to be designed in a unique way. Since that did not occur, he was almost left with nothing. Fortunately, I was able to negotiate for some payment to be made to him, but more importantly, I made sure the changes were made so that the same problem never occurred again.

Since many of my clients use versions of the same complex structure, the group benefits issue occurs quite frequently. I'm always deeply disturbed when I come across clients paying for benefits they will <u>not be able to use</u>. Therefore, I work with specialty providers who can structure the contracts to deal with more sophisticated needs for the individuals and particularly for the owners.

There are some benefits that, when you look at the owner's needs in particular, can be structured in a better way because they frequently take money in unusual ways. They work hard to pay less in taxes, and that can actually create problems for them if something goes wrong down the road. On paper, they're not making much money. For example, disability insurance is a paycheque replacer. If, on paper, you don't have a significant paycheque there may not be much to insure. Making sure that the insurance is designed in such a way that the plan takes into consideration some before-deduction dollars can go a long way to making sure that my client is adequately protected.

I've seen a lot of cases, in business environments as well as personal ones, where people make what I call inferior healthcare decisions for financial reasons. As an analogy, have you ever been so busy that you never stopped for gas and then you ran out? It ends up costing you way more time than stopping for gas ever would have done. People do the same thing for healthcare costs. They put off things. Dental work is an easy example. They don't go to the dentist and have their checkups and make sure that a small problem (a small cavity) is looked after before it becomes a big cavity and a root canal is required. Frequently, one of the reasons is financial. They say, "I don't know how much this is going to cost me, so I'm not going to go," or, "I know it's going to cost me more money than I have, so I'm not going to go."

If they have the dental plan in place, they know it's covered. They know they're going to be able to get most, if not all of it paid for. They go and they get it looked after. As a result, they don't run out of gas. They take an hour away from the office. They go get a cleaning or a filling. They come back and they're working the next day, instead of not looking after it and getting an infected tooth, which eventually gets worse and worse and worse. They're not functioning at full capacity because they're distracted by the pain of the tooth.

Then, eventually, they take the time to go see the dentist, which is several hours to have a root canal done. Then they're on pain medications and they have a day or two off work. They have medications that, when they do get back to work, may affect their productivity, etc. This is just like sitting on the side of the road waiting for a tow truck to come with a tank of gas for you. It costs you way more time and money in the long run than just going to get your tank filled in the first place would have done.

That costs the employer money too. It's not just the employee's bill for the dentist. It costs the employer when people aren't looking after themselves because it affects productivity, whether it's time or just functioning at a reduced capacity.

PART TWO - Exposing the Common Myths about Group Benefits

I'm going to expose some of the common myths about benefits plans:

Myth #1: Insurers just want your money and don't want to pay or try to get out of paying claims

This attitude comes from movies, lawyer ads, and one-sided stories we hear. It's simply not true. However, unfortunately, the level of fraud and continuous pressure to cut prices has lead Insurers of all types to look at claims more closely. Sometimes they may stick closer to the letter than your intent for your plan.

Think about it, Group Carriers don't need to decline claims since **they get to adjust your rates each year** based on what your staff has spent! In fact, it is arguable **that it is in their interest to pay as many claims as possible** since they make a "mark-up" on whatever you spend.

While it is true that some carriers seem to be more flexible than others on certain types of claims, this is generally due to a philosophical difference in how they view their role in the relationship. If they see themselves as partners with the duty to help you control costs, they are going to have tighter controls around certain types of claims in particular.

On the other hand, if they see paying claims as a way to improve their bottom line, they don't seem to be as strict. For example, one of the most common claims complaints I hear revolves around orthotics. One carrier may have strict rules regarding what qualifies and where/how you get them. Another may pay for almost anything, as long as it has a semblance of eligibility.

Would you prefer a plan that only pays for things that are truly necessary/covered, thus keeping down costs for everyone which helps keep the program viable or a plan where rates are continually increasing as claims increase because "they cover everything?"

Myth #2: Rates keep going up each year without reason

The truth is every Insurer provides detailed reports to the Broker showing exactly what you paid in premiums, what they paid out on claims by you and your staff, what they had hoped to pay, and the anticipated "inflation rate" (called their "Trend Factor"). This is what they expect their claims to go up by across ALL their groups, not just yours. Obviously they need enough money in the pot to pay everyone's claims. This is part of the "Art of group renewal analysis." These factors are the primary drivers of renewal rates.

Your broker should be communicating what rate changes are taking place for your plan, and why. They get paid a commission on renewal to provide this service.

"Dabblers" may just accept the numbers the Insurer gives while group benefits experts will analyze, negotiate on your behalf, and deliver reasonable renewal plans to you. You will not find a "take it or leave it" mindset with a specialist.

Myth #3: New brokers cut your rate to get the business but then ramp them back up the next year

This actually has some truth to it, unfortunately. If you have a great broker who shows you exactly why your rates are what they are, then obviously the only way to get a lower price would be with "unsustainable pricing" unless the new broker can explain why it is mathematically feasible.

Carriers actually do this fairly regularly hoping to make it up over time. Unless your experience is really bad or highly unpredictable, they usually will offer up to about a 10% discount just to "get the business".

On renewal, however, this translates to "poor experience", thereby justifying an increase at that point. This will be at or above what the original carrier had/would have offered that time around. If the new carrier happens to be a "pay everything" provider the renewal could be much worse. You could also have an issue switching back since staff love these plan providers.

With all that said, if your Broker has not been giving you rates clearly correlated to experience whether it's because they are not experts or because they are more focused on their own commission (commission is a percentage of premiums), your rates may have crept up when you were not looking. This does happen unfortunately. Every industry has a few bad apples.

I once had a case where I was able to get a group over 30% in reductions. Even with my special program and expertise, this should NOT HAVE been possible! This was a sure sign that the client was being overcharged by their former broker.

- ○ On the topic of "buying" business, one thing some clients have difficulty with is a new advisor asking for their past renewals including the applicable rates.

- ○ This seems counter-intuitive. After all, when you are negotiating for a new car or some other big purchase, you don't tell the second dealership what you've been quoted by the first dealership. You ask for their best price.

- ○ Sometimes, clients go further and say their existing Broker shopped the plan for them and didn't ask for that information. What these clients don't understand is that the incumbent has this information on file and sent it to the Insurers they approached!

  - ○ Since all carriers use a version of the same formula to determine rates (new and renewal), past experience + inflation + their target profit margin = renewal/new rates they need this to quote accurately. With my Architect clients I use the analogy of a site survey. They need to know what they are going to build on; they can't just provide a design as it may not suit the location!

Accordingly, prospective new carriers need to know what claims have been filed and what the rates were so they can figure out where the premiums you paid came from.

This will help them determine an appropriate rate. They may then apply a marketing discount to "try and buy the business."

- o For example I had a group where their loss experience rate was increasing. When I investigated further, I found that their claims were actually steady but premiums were down. What was happening?

It turns out that they had fewer staff members the past year but the ones that were still there were the higher claimants.

If you just showed a new carrier the year-over-year loss ratio increase, they would assume rates had to go up. If you only show the stable claims they may assume rates could stay the same or even be reduced.

Only with all the information can a reasonable rate be set.

Myth #4: You should change advisor/Insurers every few years

If you trust your advisor and understand the numbers, there is likely no benefit to moving. As you can see from what you have read so far, any new Advisor had better be able to show you something beyond simply saying, "I can save you money!"

- o There needs to be a REASON their price would be better.

    - o The Broker should also offer value-added services.

    - o They should be able to show you a sample of their renewal report to compare with what you get now. Look for substance and details! For example, if you get next to nothing right now, anything might look great. But just putting the insurance report in a pretty folder does not a good renewal package make.

○ How about interpretations of the data? Remember the increasing loss ratio with stable claims scenario I mentioned earlier?

Occasionally, an Insurer will, for their own internal reasons, cease to be competitive and not be willing to negotiate on a renewal, etc. In these rare cases, an expert broker will shop around for you. If they don't or for some reason can't, then it makes sense to look at a move. Otherwise, there should be almost no reason for you to change.

○ When considering changing due to price make sure you factor for other costs. For example:

1) Your time looking around in the first place.

2) You and/or your admin's time to get all of the forms completed, set up new systems, etc.

3) Lost productivity costs for staff time to complete the paperwork.

4) Staff will also ask questions and you will have to deal with issues that come up with the new carrier etc.

In discussing exactly this with a prospective new client at a smaller firm a while ago, we went through a process at the end of which she figured it would cost her and the company at least $2,000 to make the change I was proposing.

In the end, they still decided to work with me—I think, at least in part, because I showed them a change in program isn't always all milk and honey.

Myth #5: A new broker/insurer can get you a discount (at least for a year)

First, see Myth #3!

Second there are fewer Insurers with whom to get a discount.

Third, in addition to looking for "claims experience" information, insurers look for stability.

- After all, if they lose money the first year by buying your business, they need to keep you for at least a few years to make up for it.

If they see a habit of changing insurers, then they may refuse to quote or they quote higher to prevent you from picking them. (Yes this does happen, and not just for this reason.)

In the end, this can leave you worse off than staying put, assuming your current broker is acceptable.

Brokers that do this eventually get a reputation, too, which leads to their not getting the best rates for their existing clients. (See quoting high comment above!)

- A questionable tactic occasionally used by some brokers is to not tell prospective Insurers a client already has a plan. This can lead to significant **initial** savings for a group with high claims.

However, again the Insurers eventually figure it out. And of course, would you really want to do business with anyone that misrepresents themselves and your company this way?

I have come across a few situations over the years where an Insurer decides for some reason to ignore experience (this typically occurs with smaller groups). In this situation, a group that has high rates may save a significant amount. In these situations, I'm **obligated** to present the option. When I do, I explain it is for the upcoming year with a clear understanding that it is a "fluke" and rates will go up dramatically the next year to come back in-line.

- Some clients choose the "bird in hand" (who can blame them!) while others opt for "stability."

  - Remember as mentioned earlier, there are costs associated with making a change that are not part of the rate quoted!

- Again, this is rare, especially since the carriers can't make it up on other investments like they used to.

Again, I recommend you find a specialist!

In my profession, all a broker needs to sell group benefits is a Life Insurance Broker's license. There is no special license, training, or expertise required for one to hang out their sign as a "group benefits" broker.

Sometimes, brokers offer Group Benefits when a client who owns a business says, "Do you know anyone…?" Since there is commission involved, they may say, "Yes, Me!" I'm not saying they are doing anything wrong, they simply may not understand the levels of complexity involved in being a group benefits expert.

To provide an analogy, I do a lot of work with Architects and others in the Design Community. Through their extensive education and training they know what it takes to design just about anything.

With that said, they would admit that, if their specialization was industrial/commercial or retail, they COULD design a hospital or a Muskoka cottage, but it might not be great because it isn't what they do all the time. They might not know the "tips and tricks" needed for these types of structures.

Of course the reverse is true; a great hospital designer may not be able to design a great store.

- o Likewise, people trained overseas as Architects, Engineers, Doctors, etc. need Canadian training before they can practice here. Designing a hotel to withstand a typhoon is not the same as designing one to deal with snow and ice.

Myth #6: All Insurers are the same

Actually, this myth is becoming more and more a reality. Technology is "the great leveling field"; as one example, all carriers use computerized claims systems now.

Differentiation is getting harder. Today, when one company introduces a new technology (e.g., online claims submission), within a couple of years, everyone else has this too. Now a few have an "app", but again, the rest are not that far behind. This, combined with Insurer consolidation, has cut the number of companies offering benefits dramatically.

When I started in the 90's there were dozens of Carriers offering Group Benefits. Now there is only a handful.

This brings you back to finding a great broker to work on your behalf rather than a "better insurer" offering a better rate or plan.

Myth #7: Some Insurers are hard to deal with

Even with all the consolidation noted above no Insurer has a monopoly, at least not yet. The good news for you is that you do have choices!

Add to that the internet and people being able to say *blog, tweet, etc. about anything, any time and no company can get away with being hard to deal with!

Even the big phone and cable companies are coming around as foreign companies and technology allow smaller companies to nip at their heels. Unfortunately, turning a ship as large as those takes time. I hope, for their sake, that they can do it before it's too late, as a lot of people depend on them for jobs, pensions, etc.

Where the "difficult" label comes from, in my opinion, is that companies may look at their responsibility differently.

If a Benefits provider feels they should be helping the employer to control costs they may ask more questions, require more information, have stricter compliance, etc. for certain types of claims in particular. Others that are less strict may process similar claims with less analysis. Note: Even the strictest Carrier processes most claims without issue, i.e. 95%? 99%?

The former may get a reputation with staff, but more importantly with the service providers such as massage therapists, people that sell "orthotics," etc. as being harder to deal with compared to the other type. Of course there is a range throughout the middle. In my experience, the service providers like the "easier" ones and dislike the "more difficult." They are quick to tell staff, "That company is hard to deal with…"

Remember, the "easy to deal with" companies may pay more claims, which would lead to the employer paying higher rates, and of course their staff as well if they share in the costs.

For example, orthotics is a not uncommon issue. Depending upon whom you speak to, some say everyone would benefit from using them while others say very few people truly need them.

"Orthotics" can mean everything from Dr. Scholl's shoe inserts that you can find at any drug or grocery store, to "Proper" custom-built ones.

Orthopedic shoes range from Birkenstocks™ to handmade shoes to deal with a significant problem. As an example, my stepfather Jim used to be one of those shoemakers. Back in the 70s and 80s he worked at Sunnybrook Hospital in Toronto. I remember him talking about making a pair for a veteran. The Vet had been shot in the leg. As a result it was a couple of inches shorter than the other one. He built one shoe with a thinner soul and the other with a thick one to compensate. No one would question the need for something like that.

Another area of issue may have nothing to do with the plan or the employee. Unfortunately, some service providers act questionable if not fraudulently. Everything from recommending more services than are really needed to billing under a different family member than the one they treated to giving people a kickback if they let them over bill the insurer!

When a claim comes through from a provider that has been flagged by the insurer, even legitimate ones can be delayed or require additional documentation, etc. I recently received a notice from a provider that they were no longer paying claims from a certain provider and that in fact had reported the provider to the police who had laid charges!

Myth #8: Some Carriers offer better coverage than others

With the exception of "package plans," that some organizations offer, this is not true.

When I hear a comment like this it is generally from someone that was covered by a plan at a large organization.

The truth is the Carriers do have some limits (sometimes determined by the size of the group) however, the business owner has the real control over design! For example:

- What percentage of the different types of claims will the plan cover? 80%? 100%?

- Will there be a deductible? (this is an amount the employee has to pay before the plan pays)

- Should there be a drug card or should the employees have to submit for reimbursement?

- Will there be coverage for glasses and contacts?

  o How much?

- Which "Paramedical Providers" will be covered? Most cover Chiro, Physio, massage, etc., but what about Social Workers (generally as Family Councillors), Osteopaths, Athletic Therapists, Christian Science Practitioners, etc.

  o What coverage limits will apply to these?

  o Will some have higher limits than others?

  o Will some of these require a Doctor's note?

- Will "Lifestyle" treatments for smoking cessation, weight loss, and erectile dysfunction be covered?

- How about Fertility Treatments? These are very costly and for those that need them they are very important! What does the employer feel is their responsibility related to such?

- For Dental the same percentage and dollar limit questions apply but also what types of treatments are covered? All plans generally cover, check-ups, cleanings, fillings and extractions, Periodontics (Gum Disease Treatments) and Endodontics (Root Canals) but what about:

  o "Cosmetic" treatments like crowns, bridges, dentures or the real biggee, Implants?

  o Orthodontics is another big one (read expensive!). If you do offer it, do you cover adults too (there is a big trend towards this, these days!) or only "children" (under 18)?

Whatever the limits are in your current plan, someone put them there. They may be a carryover from the past.

For example, all drug plans were once "reimbursement." That is, you pay at the pharmacy then mail in your receipt to get your money back.

This is no longer the case as all providers offer drug cards. You may choose to stay with reimbursement, but it IS a choice.

There may have been an overt decision made at some point to help control costs, e.g. requiring a Doctor's note for massage therapy.

These are not Insurer-imposed. You can usually remove or modify any such requirements, increase many of the limits, etc. However, there will likely be an immediate cost and of course easier access to more coverage will usually lead to more usage which may mean another increase at renewal. (The initial increase the insurer quotes is an educated guess. If your claims are higher or lower than their guess, your rates will be adjusted at renewal. NOTE: they cannot make any rate changes mid-term no matter how high claims may go!)

With that said, when you take the "Benefits as an Investment" approach, it could be worthwhile. For example, if getting regular massages keeps people at their computers for longer periods of time, with fewer breaks, sick days, etc. due to tension headaches, the increase in productivity may be worth higher premiums!

The key, as with any Investment, is understanding and balancing the risk you are willing to take. A key to help you with this is education. (Like reading this book!) I once had an employee at a firm try to claim a new mattress for his bad back. While I empathized with him and his problem, most would agree paying for a bed is going too far. Covering everything would be nice but we know the cost would be too great even without any fraud and abuse.

Accordingly, each client needs to review their individual needs and budget to find a solution that suits them.

Remember that renewal process I mentioned earlier? In addition to looking at experience and rates, it is a good idea to look at your plan design itself, in detail, at least every couple of years. I don't just mean a bad year with an eye to cutting coverage to cut costs. That may be necessary to protect the majority of employees and the viability of the plan; however coverage reduction should always be a last resort! The staff fallout may cost more than the rate increase!

If it is necessary to reduce coverage, I suggest educating staff about what is happening and why first. If you do have to cut back, an educated staff will accept it more willingly than if they think, "The boss or the Insurer just decided it arbitrarily" or "only did it to increase profits, etc."

"It's Insurance Not Rocket Science!"

I actually had an admin person at a prospective client business say this to me years ago. This comment was quickly followed by "just give me a quote." If you have read this far, I hope you recognize that, while it may not be rocket science, there is science (and art) to making sure YOUR Benefits plan is appropriate to your needs and your budget.

Want to know what happened with the "rocket scientist" prospect? After unsuccessfully trying to connect with the principal directly and a few attempts to educate the admin person, I politely declined to proceed further. To the best of my knowledge, they still have no plan in place. How do I know this? I keep running into their former staff at other firms I work with who tell me that not having a plan is one of the reasons people keep leaving there.

In Summary….Exposing the Most Common Mistakes, and How to Avoid Them

Here are the most common mistakes I see business owners and key players make with their group benefits and some tips about what you can do:

- Not understanding how their rates are determined.

    o Make sure you are getting information about renewals and that you understand how it is used to set your rates for the coming year.

- Having an adversarial approach with their Insurer/Broker.

    o If you are unsatisfied with something related to your plan or claims, don't assume you have a bad plan or carrier. Ask your advisor or even go directly to the Insurer's service team with concerns.

    In today's competitive world, there really are no bad carriers. They all have computerized claims handling, so only possible fraud or clearly not-covered claims are ever even looked at, let alone declined.

- Too much distance between the Broker/Carrier and the Business Owner/Decision Maker.

○ Dealing with the Group Plan is rarely considered a high payoff activity for the business owner. Especially once they have made the decision to proceed with a plan they tend to want to leave everything to an Admin person. These may be very qualified people however they are not the owners. Ideally, the Owner, CFO, etc. participates in the renewal process each year but at least every couple of years. This prevents a disconnect from their only seeing the balance sheet line entry and asking "why is this costing so much more than last year…" The per-person costs might actually be down but if the company has grown & hired a lot more staff the amount being paid out could be much higher. With the growth might come new needs, e.g. to compete against another larger firm you might need to add coverage, add a RRSP/Pension Plan, etc. to attract and keep top people from your other large competitors.

- Make sure you are getting expert advice. Does your broker:

  - Specialize in group coverage or just dabble in it?

  - Give you details or just rates at renewal?

  - Stay in touch throughout the year to make sure your staff members are satisfied with claims handling?

  - Warn you of pending issues that could affect your renewal or wait to surprise you with a rate hike?

If you are new to group or if you don't have complete confidence in your Broker, shop around before to find a Broker that is right for you!

There are many more Brokers than there are Insurers to choose from. Ask people you know, search online, and look for someone who specializes in your business.

- Some associations, etc., have special plans. These may offer preferred rates and coverages vs. being a "stand alone" business.

- It is most important that your broker knows your industry and has more at stake when dealing with you than just your company.

Interested in My Help?

To get started, you can contact my office at 1-800-446-5745. My staff will set you up with an appointment to speak with me. We'll discuss what your needs are, which is different from a conversation about "what you currently have." We'll discuss any special circumstances with any issues that you've heard about from within your team, etc.

We can even discuss new trends and ideas that you may have heard about. Some are good, others are like many things, more hype than substance. As business owners know, there is no such thing as a "free lunch" when it comes to running their companies. There are ways to reduce costs but a proper cost/benefit analysis must be done. You cannot just accept what you hear.

If necessary, we'll then work with clients to redesign the plan as needed. Once your plan is finalized and set up, we always do a presentation to make sure staff knows exactly what they have available to them but also what the implications of using them are. We find that when employees understand "Benefits 101" and buy in to why and how their program works the plan runs more efficiently and costs usually stabilize.

Finally, every year at renewal I go through detailed reports explaining to clients exactly what they paid, what was paid out on their behalf, and how that impacts what they're going to pay in the subsequent year.

We also monitor their plan throughout the year. If I see something starting to go off side, i.e. claims have gone way up—we touch base with them straightaway, rather than waiting until renewal time and hitting them with an unforeseen increase. This is preferable to our showing up at the anniversary and saying, "Oh, by the way, we're increasing your rates fifty percent." Did you ever notice it's a lot easier to swallow something painful when you had a bit of a warning? I always prefer to be proactive.

About the Author

Douglas Pinnell is an insurance veteran who has spent nearly two decades in insurance, gaining expertise in life insurance, living benefits, and health and dental programs.

He is a sought-after speaker on wealth and business preservation topics such as succession planning and maximizing investment in a group benefits plan. Pinnell also serves on boards such as the Society for Design Administration and CSC's Grand Valley Chapter.

Douglas is part of a husband-and-wife insurance team with more than 45 years of combined experience. The insurance veterans have helped Mumby Insurance Brokers reach new heights of innovation while maintaining a client-centered approach. Douglas's business partner Anthea Mumby publishes *The Mumby Report* and *Business by Design*—free educational newsletters available to clients and others interested in maximizing their insurance dollar.

Having grown up in Parry Sound Ontario, with his first boat at the age of 10, Douglas is happiest on the water, and is an avid boater.

How Great Is Your Group Benefits Package?

Your Group Benefits Readiness Assessment

Circle the statement which is most true for you:

1. We are able to recruit top talent as a direct result of our benefits program:

- Yes: It's one of our key differentiators: 10 points

- No: We lose out to our competition: 0 points

- Unknown: Unsure whether or not our benefits have an effect: 5 points

Score: _____

2. I have a comprehensive review of my group benefits program:

- Every Year: 10 points

- Every few years: 5 points

- As far as I know, never: 0 points

Score: _____

3. Our staff morale is above average and turnover is below average for our industry:

- True: 10 points
- False: 5 points

Score: _____

4. I fully understand where our group benefits money goes each year (See Myth # 2):

- Yes, we get detailed reports and understand why rates increase: 10 points
- No, we are in the dark about why our rates just keep increasing: 0 points

Score: _____

5. Do you see your group benefits plan as an investment or an expense? Be honest!

- Investment—We know we get back more in value: 10 points
- Expense—It's a necessary evil: 0 points

Score: _____

6. Myth # 8 spoke about plan design. Do you know where your design came from and are you happy with it?

- Yes to both: 10 points
- Yes to one: 5 points
- No to both: 0 points

    Score: _____

7. Our employees are engaged and fully understand our benefits program:

- Yes: 10 points
- No: 5 points

Score: _____

8. I understand the many tax and liability implications related to my group benefits program:

- Yes: 10 points
- No: 0 points

    Score: _____

9. I understand that claim issues are inevitable and they may not always be resolved the way I like. When they have happened:

- They were resolved or if they weren't I understood why (The claim was higher than the plan limit):
    - Yes: 3 points
    - No: 0 points
- I had to resolve it myself:
    - Yes: 0 points
    - No: 2 points
- I know I can immediately call my advisor to deal with it:
    - Yes: 5 points
    - No: 0 points

    Score: _____

10. I am eligible for and take advantage of any special coverages and/or discounts available through my profession:

- I am eligible:
    - Yes: 5 points
    - No: 0 Points
- I am taking advantage of these discounts:
    - Yes: 5 points
    - No: 0 points

How did you do?

- Below 65: Your Company is a textbook candidate for an overhaul of your group benefits plan and you should move quickly to improve yours or establish one.

- 65–80: Your Company is bound to have some improvements to your bottom line with a comprehensive review of your benefits plan. You should move quickly to review yours.

- 80–90: Your Company is doing well. However, there may be a few key areas where you could improve your bottom line. You should call to review your benefits program soon.

- 90–100: Your Company is doing a lot of things right. You might still consider exploring the option of having us take a look at your benefits program as it's always a good idea to get a fresh set of eyes on your program to ensure you are not leaving any money on the table. Give us a call to review your benefits program before your next renewal is up.

For more help with this assessment, call my office at 1-800-446-5745, or email me at douglas@mumby.com.